Hard work ins't the problem

A.M. Dyer

Copyright © 2026 by A.M. Dyer

All rights reserved.

No portion of this book may be reproduced in any form without written permission from the publisher or author, except as permitted by U.S. copyright law.

Contents

1. Chapter 1   1
   Why Hard Work Isn't the Problem
2. Chapter 2   3
   Persistence vs Progress
3. Chapter 3   5
   Systems Decide Outcomes
4. Chapter 4   7
   The Ceiling Problem
5. Chapter 5   9
   Leverage: The Effort Multiplier
6. Chapter 6   11
   Busy Is Not the Same as Progress
7. Chapter 7   13
   Identity and the Struggle Loop
8. Chapter 8   15
   Skills That Compound
9. Chapter 9   17
   Decisions Beat Intensity

10.	Chapter 10 Ownership Changes the Game	19
11.	Chapter 11 Environment Is Strategy	21
12.	Chapter 12 Effort With Intent	23
13.	Conclusion Aim Your Effort	25

Chapter One

Chapter 1

Hard work matters. Nothing meaningful happens without effort. Skills don't appear on their own. Bills don't pay themselves. No one accidentally builds a good life by waiting around.

But hard work does not guarantee success.

Plenty of people do everything they're told. They show up early, stay late, take responsibility, and keep pushing. Years pass, and nothing changes. Same stress. Same ceiling. Still living paycheck to paycheck.

They aren't lazy.

They aren't incapable.

They aren't "doing it wrong".

They're applying effort inside systems that don't reward it.

Most of us were raised on a simple promise: work hard, keep your head down, and things will work out. It feels fair. It feels earned. It suggests the world rewards effort predictably.

The problem is that effort and outcomes are not automatically linked.

If hard work alone guaranteed success, the hardest-working people would be the wealthiest. They aren't. Some of the most exhausted people you'll ever meet are also the most stuck. Tradespeople with broken bodies. Professionals buried under responsibility. Business owners who are grinding seven days a week just to stay afloat.

The issue isn't effort.
It's where that effort is aimed.

Effort is fuel. You don't go anywhere without it. But fuel doesn't decide the destination — direction does. You can have a full tank and still be driving in circles.

When effort is applied to something that grows, it compounds.
When it's applied to something capped, it plateaus.
When it's applied to something broken, it burns you out.

Most people were never taught how to evaluate where their effort goes. They were taught to endure. To push through. To assume that if something isn't working, the answer must be more effort.

That belief keeps people loyal to struggle, instead of being loyal to the outcomes.

Hard work isn't the problem. Treating it like a recipe for success is.
Effort is the starting point — not the plan.

Chapter Two

Chapter 2

Persistence sounds noble.

We're taught to stick it out. Push through. Don't quit. Keep grinding. In the right context, that advice is valuable. In the wrong one, it quietly costs people years of their lives.

Because endurance and progress are not the same thing.

Endurance means you can keep going.

Progress means something is actually changing.

Many people endure a great deal while going nowhere. They tolerate long hours, stress, and responsibility gets added year after year, only to look up and realise their position hasn't improved — except they're more tired than they used to be.

From the outside, it looks admirable.

From the inside, it feels like being stuck on a treadmill.

Most people don't persist because things are improving. They persist because stopping feels like failure.

Once you've invested time, energy, and identity into a path, walking away feels like admitting it was all for nothing. The longer you stay, the harder it becomes to leave — not because it's working, but because you've tied your self-worth to seeing it through.

So effort doubles down. Not strategically, but emotionally.

This is how persistence turns into a trap.

Burnout isn't a weakness. It's feedback.

It's your nervous system recognising that your effort is no longer producing returns. The work may be constant, even intense, but nothing is improving. No momentum. No leverage. No sense of movement.

Pushing harder doesn't solve that problem. It accelerates it.

When effort only keeps things from falling apart — paying bills, meeting deadlines, holding ground — the brain shifts into survival mode. Growth stress can be energising. Survival stress is draining. Stay there long enough, and burnout is inevitable.

Quitting gets a bad reputation, but quitting the wrong thing is often the smartest move available.

Stopping doesn't erase the value of past effort. Skills transfer. Experience compounds. What you're walking away from isn't the work — it's the assumption that this particular path must be honored forever.

Strong people don't persist blindly. They persist intelligently.

They reassess. They redirect. They stop before exhaustion makes the decision for them.

Persistence is powerful when progress exists — when learning continues, When tangible benefits are seen, and effort builds something that grows.

When signs of progress disappear, persistence stops being discipline and becomes loyalty to the struggle.

And struggle, on its own, doesn't owe you anything.

Chapter Three

Chapter 3

Effort does not exist in a vacuum.

No matter how motivated or disciplined you are, your results are shaped by the system you're operating inside. That system quietly decides what effort is rewarded, what effort is ignored, and what effort is punished.

This isn't about excuses.

It's about mechanics.

A system is simply the environment that turns effort into outcomes.

It includes how work is valued, who owns the profits of your labor, how advancement happens, and where limits are set. Every job, industry, and business has a system — even if no one ever explains it to you.

Motivation determines how much energy you apply.

Systems determine what that energy becomes.

In a strong system, effort compounds. Skills stack. Progress builds on itself. Even slow growth feels like movement.

In a weak system, effort gets absorbed. You work harder just to maintain your position. Progress is capped regardless of commitment.

That's why you can find capable, driven people completely stuck — and others moving ahead with far less visible effort. The difference isn't character. It's return.

We like to pretend everyone's playing the same game.

They're not.

Some systems offer clear pathways, transferable skills, and benefits that grow with the value created. Others offer stability, predictability, and hard limits. Neither is inherently good or bad — but confusing one for the other creates frustration.

Telling people in both environments to "just work harder" ignores the fact that the rules are different.

In weak systems, extra effort often gets praised but not rewarded in a way that changes the long-term picture. You become valuable — but replaceable. Busy — but capped. Needed — but stuck.

When outcomes fall short, people are taught to look inward.

"I need to be more disciplined."

"I need to push harder."

"I need to improve myself."

Rarely are they encouraged to ask whether the system is designed to reward extra effort at all.

Systems aren't moral. They're structural.

Some are built for growth. Some are built for stability. Some quietly extract more than they give back. The mistake isn't choosing a system — it's misunderstanding its limits.

Once you see the system clearly, effort stops being wasted. You can decide whether to stay, adapt, or reposition. Awareness doesn't remove responsibility — it sharpens it.

Because effort still matters.

But structure decides what effort becomes.

Chapter Four

Chapter 4

Most people don't fail because they lack effort.
They stall because the path they're on has a ceiling — and no one ever told them where it was.

A ceiling is the maximum outcome a structure allows, regardless of how hard you work. Once you reach it, progress slows, then stops. Effort continues, but returns flatten.

Time-based income is the most common example.

When hours equal money, growth is capped by how much time and energy you can physically supply. Early on, effort clearly pays off. Work more, earn more. Over time, the curve flattens. Raises shrink. Hours stretch. The ceiling quietly approaches.

By the time most people notice it, they're already trapped under it.

Ceilings are often disguised as advancement.

More responsibility. Bigger workloads. More people are relying on you. The work feels more important — but the upside stays roughly the same. That's not growth. It's pressure dressed up as progress.

This is where confusion sets in. People assume the problem is effort. So they push harder. They take on more. They sacrifice more.

But effort is additive.

Ceilings are structural.

No amount of discipline breaks a system that wasn't designed to reward extra contribution.

Hitting a ceiling rarely feels dramatic. It shows up as restlessness. Frustration. A constant sense of being busy but stuck. Motivation fades because the brain recognises that extra effort no longer changes the outcome.

This is where burnout often begins — not because the work is hard, but because it no longer leads anywhere.

Ceilings aren't failures.

Some ceilings provide stability, predictability, and security — things that matter at certain stages of life. The problem is expecting unlimited outcomes from limited structures.

Once you see the ceiling, you regain choice.

You can accept it.

Plan around it.

Or move toward something else.

What matters is knowing it's there.

Effort works best when it's aligned with structure — or deliberately moving beyond it.

Chapter Five

Chapter 5

If effort is fuel, leverage is like the tires on your car; without them, you won't go far.

Without leverage, effort is linear. You work, you get paid, and tomorrow you start again from zero. Stop working, and everything stops with you. That's the default setting for most jobs and most people.

Leverage changes that equation.

Leverage allows effort to keep working after you stop. It turns work from something that expires into something that compounds.

This isn't a trick or a buzzword. Leverage is simply anything that reduces the direct link between time spent and value created.

When leverage is present, progress stacks. Options increase. When it isn't, effort resets daily.

There are several forms of leverage.

Transferable skills are the most accessible. Some skills are narrow and easily replaced. Others travel across roles and industries, stacking with experience and making it harder to box them in. These skills quietly multiply the value of everything else you do.

Capital is stored effort. Money, assets, and resources allow effort to be applied indirectly. Capital works without getting tired. It removes time as the main constraint.

Ownership is where leverage really accelerates. When you don't own what you build, effort produces fixed rewards. When you do, effort gains momentum. The same work suddenly matters more because the result compounds.

Systems and technology scale effort. A process, tool, or platform allows one person's work to reach far beyond their own capacity.

Delegation multiplies outcomes by removing personal bottlenecks. Work shared effectively grows faster than work carried alone.

Leverage often feels disappointing at first.

It requires setup, learning, and patience. Early effort doesn't produce immediate feedback, which is why many people retreat to grinding away. Grinding feels productive. Leverage feels slow — until it isn't.

Effort without leverage keeps you alive.
Effort with leverage builds options.

Leverage doesn't replace work.
It makes work worth doing.

Chapter Six

Chapter 6

One of the easiest traps to fall into is confusing activity with advancement.

Being busy feels productive. Tasks get completed. Emails get answered. Days fill up. There's constant motion, and motion creates the feeling that something is happening.

But busyness and progress are not the same thing.

Busyness provides instant feedback. Your brain gets a small reward every time something is crossed off the list. Progress is slower and quieter. It often involves thinking, planning, learning, or setting things up that won't pay off immediately.

Because progress doesn't shout, many people avoid it.

You can become extremely efficient at maintaining your position without improving it. Productivity tools and routines make this worse when they optimise the wrong work. Doing more of the wrong things faster doesn't fix the problem — it locks it in.

Maintenance work has value. It keeps things running. But when all your effort goes into maintenance, nothing changes. You stay afloat, but you don't move ahead.

Progress is directional. It answers a simple question:

If this works, what actually changes?

If the answer is "not much", the work is probably keeping you busy rather than moving you forward.

Busyness is often a form of avoidance. Activity fills the space where uncomfortable questions live. Questions like whether the path makes sense, or what happens if nothing changes.

Days stay full. Weeks blur. Years pass.

Progress rarely looks impressive in the moment. Learning a new skill. Building a system. Positioning for future opportunity. None of it comes with urgency or applause — but over time, it quietly reshapes your options.

Busyness creates motion.
Progress creates movement.

The difference is direction.

Chapter Seven

Chapter 7

For many people, effort isn't just something they do.
It's who they are.

They're the reliable ones. The hard worker. The person who always shows up, stays late, and gets things done. That identity brings pride and security — and, in many environments, it's the only recognition on offer.

It's also where the trap forms.

When effort becomes identity, questioning direction feels personal. Slowing down feels like weakness. Changing course feels like failure. So instead of reassessing, people double down. They carry more. Push harder. Stay longer.

Not because it works — but because it protects who they believe they are.

Over time, loyalty shifts. Instead of being loyal to outcomes — growth, stability, freedom — people become loyal to effort itself. As long as they're working hard, it feels justified, even if nothing improves.

Struggle turns into proof of value.

This is why people stay in roles, businesses, and routines that stopped serving them years ago. Effort becomes the reason to stay, not the tool to move forward.

Being busy looks responsible. Being exhausted looks committed. Being calm and strategic can look like you're not trying hard enough — even when you're doing the most important work of all.

So effort becomes a performance rather than being applied wisely.

Escaping this loop requires separating worth from workload.

Your value is not measured by how much you carry.

Your character is not proven by exhaustion.

Effort is a resource, not a moral obligation.

Letting go of struggle isn't erasing the past. Skills transfer. Experience compounds. What you're releasing is the belief that suffering is required to justify progress.

Identity should support outcomes — not trap you in place.

Chapter Eight

Chapter 8

Effort improves performance.
Skills shape opportunity.

You can work extremely hard and still end up boxed in if the skills you're developing don't travel, don't scale, or don't stay relevant. That's not a failure of work ethic — it's a mismatch between effort and return.

Most people learn skills reactively. They focus on what's required for the role in front of them, not what will still matter five or ten years down the track. That works — until the environment changes.

Some skills age poorly.

They're tightly tied to specific tools, systems, or roles. You can become very good at them and still hit a ceiling because their value depends entirely on where you're standing.

Other skills compound.

Compounding skills increase in value over time. They transfer across industries, stack with experience, and improve decision-making. They don't just make you better at your current role — they expand your options.

Examples include:

- Clear communication
- Problem-solving
- Financial understanding
- Systems thinking
- Learning how to learn

These skills rarely come with instant recognition. They don't feel urgent. They don't always look impressive while you're building them. But over time, they quietly multiply the impact of everything else you do.

This is why skill choice is strategic.

Passion gets a lot of attention, but demand determines value. Enjoyment matters, but it doesn't override usefulness. A skill that solves problems people care about will keep opening doors long after novelty wears off.

You don't need to be exceptional at one thing. Most people do better by stacking several high-value skills that work together. Skill stacks are difficult to copy. They turn average ability into uncommon leverage.

Effort follows skill choice.

Choose skills that compound, and effort keeps paying you back. Choose skills that stall, and effort eventually plateaus with them.

Chapter Nine

Chapter 9

Effort determines how hard you push.
Decisions determine where you end up.

Most people spend their energy optimising effort — longer hours, better routines, higher productivity. Meanwhile, a small number of quiet decisions are shaping years of outcomes in the background.

You can work incredibly hard and still lose ground if that effort is misdirected.

Intensity increases speed. Direction determines destination. If the direction is wrong, effort just gets you there faster — tired and confused about how you arrived.

A handful of decisions matters more than thousands of busy days.

Which environment do you choose?

Which skills do you build?

Do you own or rent your effort?

These are directional decisions. Once made, they create momentum. Effort then amplifies them — for better or worse.

Many people don't actively choose their path. They inherit it.

They take what's available. Stay because it feels responsible. Say yes because it's expected. None of these choices is wrong — but they are still choices, even if they don't feel like it.

Default decisions feel safe. They rarely feel strategic.

Thinking gets avoided because it feels unproductive. There's no immediate output. No visible progress. Just uncertainty. So people stay busy instead — even when busyness locks in a poor direction.

One good decision, made early enough, can outperform years of grinding.

Effort matters.

But effort applied without direction multiplies mistakes just as efficiently as it multiplies success when directed correctly.

Chapter Ten

Chapter 10

Ownership changes how effort behaves.

When you rent your effort, rewards are fixed. You work, you get paid, and the transaction ends there. Do more, and you might get a little more — but the benefits are capped by the structure.

When you own part of the outcome, effort compounds.

Ownership aligns effort with results. It rewards patience, quality, and long-term thinking. Work stops feeling like expenditure and starts feeling like an investment.

This is why two people can put in similar effort and end up in completely different places. One rents their contribution. The other owns what they're building.

Ownership isn't all-or-nothing.

It exists on a spectrum:

- Equity in a business
- Income-producing assets (rental property)
- Intellectual property
- Systems you control
- A reputation you own

Each step toward ownership increases leverage. Even small amounts matter over time.

Ownership involves risk. There's no avoiding that. But avoiding all risk has a cost too — stagnation, fixed outcomes, limited upside.

The real question isn't whether ownership is risky.
It's whether the risk is intentional and aligned with what you're trying to build.

Ownership rarely pays quickly.

Early effort often looks unrewarded. Progress feels slow. Results are uneven. This is where many people retreat to renting efforts because at least it feels predictable.

Those who stick with ownership long enough benefit from compounding. Work done years earlier keeps paying today. Momentum replaces strain.

Ownership doesn't shout.
But over time, it quietly separates outcomes.

Effort alone keeps things running.
Effort plus ownership builds something that lasts.

Chapter Eleven

Chapter 11

Most people try to change themselves before they question their environment.

More discipline. Better habits. Stronger motivation. When progress stalls, the instinct is almost always to push harder from the inside.

What often gets ignored is the thing shaping behaviour the most:

The environment.

The environment determines what effort is rewarded, ignored, or punished. It sets the incentives — and incentives shape behaviour far more reliably than willpower ever will.

You can be capable, motivated, and disciplined, but if the environment caps outcomes, effort eventually hits a wall.

This is why willpower runs out. You're fighting the rules instead of working with them.

Some environments reward learning, ownership, and long-term thinking. Others reward visibility, compliance, and constant activity. People adapt to what gets rewarded — not because they're weak, but because that's how humans work.

Trying to win in an environment that isn't designed to reward the outcome you want creates frustration. Some games can't be won, no matter how hard you play them.

Leaving an environment often feels like failure.

Time has been invested. Relationships built. Rules learned. Walking away feels risky and disloyal — even when staying guarantees stagnation.

But staying in the wrong environment isn't commitment.
It's inertia.

There is no perfect environment. Every system has trade-offs: stability versus outcome, certainty versus growth, comfort versus opportunity.

Strategy isn't about avoiding limits.
It's about choosing which limits you're willing to live with.

When environment and goals align, effort feels lighter. Progress becomes visible. Burnout loosens its grip.

Choosing the right environment is one of the highest-leverage decisions you'll ever make.

Chapter Twelve

Chapter 12

Hard work isn't the issue.
Unintentional hard work is.

When effort lacks intent, everything feels urgent. Emails, requests, problems, and other people's priorities all compete for attention. Effort gets scattered across dozens of small fires, none of which meaningfully change direction.

Intent narrows the field.

It clarifies what matters, what doesn't, and what progress actually looks like. Effort stops being reactive and becomes selective. Work turns from a reflex into a choice.

Intent answers three questions:

What am I trying to change?
What does progress look like?
How will I know this is working?

Without clear answers, effort drains energy. With them, even difficult work feels lighter — not because it's easy, but because it makes sense.

Effort with intent creates feedback.

Instead of assuming work is valuable because it's hard, you evaluate whether it produces movement. Learning. Leverage. Optionality. These are better signals than hours worked or tasks completed.

Feedback allows adjustment before burnout forces it.

Energy isn't sustained by discipline alone. It's sustained by progress, autonomy, and alignment. When effort consistently leads somewhere, motivation returns naturally. When it doesn't, no amount of grit can fake it for long.

Urgency reacts.
Intent chooses.

Effort guided by intent doesn't mean doing less. It means doing what matters — and leaving the rest undone without guilt.

That's how hard work becomes sustainable.

Chapter Thirteen

Conclusion

Hard work matters.

It always has. Nothing meaningful is built without effort, discipline, and persistence. But effort alone is not a strategy.

Effort multiplies the path it's applied to when that path has room to grow; effort compounds. When it doesn't, effort exhausts.

The promise that hard work guarantees success is incomplete. It ignores systems, ceilings, leverage, ownership, timing, and environment. It places responsibility where control doesn't always exist — and encourages people to push harder instead of positioning better.

This doesn't remove responsibility.

It sharpens it.

Responsibility includes choosing direction.

Responsibility includes recognising limits.

Responsibility includes changing course when reality demands it.

Hard work is the starting point.

Direction is the plan.

Structure is the constraint.

Leverage is the multiplier.

The goal was never to work less.

It was to work toward something that grows.

Choose the direction first.

Then apply effort.

That's how hard work stops feeling like sacrifice without return — and starts building something that lasts.

www.ingramcontent.com/pod-product-compliance
Lightning Source LLC
Chambersburg PA
CBHW022023290426
44109CB00015B/1287